To Craig, Cameron, Hannah, and Ryan, who loved me through
isolation and sickness, when this story came to me as a gift for my heart.
Thank you for being family - I would choose you as friends if we weren't.

And to those who need a friend to sit with, listen to, and walk with you
through hard times. I pray you will find a friend who loves you like this.

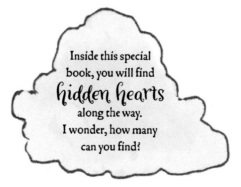

Karen xxxxx

To my dear Lenny and Beau,
Know that you always have a friend in your Auntie Lori.
To talk with, to laugh with, to pray with, and cry with.

Lori

Sincere appreciation to our creative team:
Editors: Bobbie Hinman/Mindy Kiker
Cover Design: Ellie Boultwood
Formatters: Ellie Boultwood/Amanda Letcher
Thank you sincerely precious creatives.
We couldn't have done it without your expertise, skills, and care.

Inside this special
book, you will find
hidden hearts
along the way.
I wonder, how many
can you find?

The Little Black Cloud

Karen Brough
Lori Boag

We headed outside one fine sunny day...

Right up in the sky, the clouds came to play.

Amid the white clouds, soft, light, and fluffy,

was a lone little cloud…

dark, heavy…

and snuffly.

The next thing that happened, surprising to think,

the little black cloud began to

droop

…and to

sink.

Low,
 Low,
  Low, he sank deep down below.

Til his bottom went

THUMP,

on the ground with a blow.

A friend sat beside asking, "Are you okay?"

The little black cloud, full—with so much to say.

The little black cloud, feeling *safe* with his friend,
opened his mouth to speak, and tears came instead.

The friend simply *listened* and held the cloud tight,
all the while knowing he soon would be light.

He talked, and he wept from his *heart* and his *head.*

His friend simply listened—and finally said:

"I want you to know, I want you to see.
You are loved…you are cared for…

You have a friend
here in me.

His friend then reached down to pick something up.

Was it a bowl,

a spoon,

or even a cup?

His friend showed him a bottle,

and showing his name, whispered

"This is for tears;

....now that's why I came."

"Tears are important,

don't toss them away...

They need
to come out

and
**have their
say.**

"Those tears won't be wasted,

or wonder what to do,

I'll collect them right here

in this bottle for you!"

"So you know I love you,

and alone you'll not be,

Because I love you...

you are cared for...

you have a friend

here in
me."

As time went along and he shared with his friend,
feeling no need to carry, as his heart was on the mend.

He found without rush, scurry, hard or big feel,
his insides indeed were beginning to heal.

He poured out his **worries**, all that kept him low.

His **heavies** came out ...

his sad and lonely did go.

His **black** became **grey** and then turned to *white*.

The more he let go,

the more he took *flight.*

As he shared with his friend,
he felt a lot lighter,

and little by little, he beamed so much brighter.

The little white cloud set to lift and to *fly*…

Higher and higher he went UP in the sky.

No longer heavy or glum down below,

he dipped, and he soared, felt his happiness grow.

A day can change quickly from heavy and sad,

turn into sweetness and a day to be glad!

If you are heavy, sad, or alone in your space,
there is a *friend* who sits with you
right here—in this place.

He'll collect all your tears, and that isn't the end,
because…

you are *loved*…
you are *cared for*…

...and never without a friend.

Author

Karen Brough is an award-winning author and former teacher from Australia, who writes with a teacher's heart for adults and children. She published the 'Be Held by Him' six book series for adults and is helping many navigate grief through her endorsed by health care professionals, children's grief book, 'I Can't Believe They're Gone.'

Karen sees it as a privilege to write stories that touch the heart, offering a little love, kindness, and hope to those who need it most. 'The Little Black Cloud' remains a source of comfort for her during sad moments, and she prays that readers will accept this hope investment from her heart to theirs.

Karen, her husband Craig, and their three children, along with the charismatic groodle pup Gracie, live on a semi-rural property, where she endeavors to draw near to peace and wonder as often as she can.

Illustrator

Lori Boag is a multidisciplinary artist with a passion for drawing that traces back to her early years. Her creative journey has been shaped by a fascination with fairytales, Japanese kawaii culture, and fashion. Exploring diverse mediums such as oil painting, graphite, Fimo clay sculpture, and miniature-scale landscapes has allowed Lori to bring her visions to life.

A graduate of the Lygon Street Illustration Academy in 2015, Lori has dedicated herself to the world of illustration ever since. She currently works as a learning support facilitator at Hillcrest Christian College, where she leverages her illustrative skills to help children comprehend complex concepts through visually engaging imagery, giving them a voice through expressive drawings.

The Story Behind the Story

Karen caught a nasty bug and had to stay away from her family for a long while. This meant there were no family dinners together or cuddly hugs, and this made her feel a little lonely. On her way to see the doctor, Karen noticed something strange in the sky. It was a bright sunny day and all the white clouds gathered together, but there was one little black cloud all by itself. And this made her wonder...

What was he doing here on this sunny day? Did he feel lonely all by himself? Was he weighed down by the rain within? Was he lonely? Did the white clouds notice he was feeling sad?

The next day, as Karen ate breakfast, she thought about how much she missed hugs, and eating meals with her family – this made her feel a little sad and she wept. She remembered a story about our tears being collected in a bottle and decided to try and draw this in her sketchbook. As she coloured and drew the tear bottle, she also thought about the lone little black cloud, these two ideas began to connect in her heart.

An idea suddenly popped into her mind, "Let's write the Little Black Cloud!" This sounded like fun to her, so she began writing all her thoughts down on paper. The more Karen wrote, the better she felt. Ideas and words began flowing from her pen to paper, the story poured out of her heart. Before she knew it, the morning sun was gone, and the afternoon clouds had rolled in – and a first draft of the little black cloud was written.

Yes, she was still unwell, but she didn't feel so sad, or so lonely. Writing this story was healing. To her, the Little Black Cloud became almost as real as that lone little black cloud in the sunny sky. It helped to know that others felt the same as she did at that time.

And like most nasty bugs, it soon passed, and she was able to hug her family and have family dinners together once again. Her sad and lonely days had turned into a story that helped people know they were not alone, and that they were loved. She hopes that it helps you too. Have you ever turned a sad experience into something creative? How did it make you feel?

Have You Read Our Other Titles?

Explore more heartwarming stories from our collection.
Each book is crafted with care to inspire and delight young readers.

Register for Latest Release Updates

Stay connected with us and be the first to know about new releases,
special offers, and exclusive content. https://karenbrough.com/register/

Enhance the adventure

with a Free Workbook!

Dive deeper into the lessons and hugs of "The Little Black Cloud" with our free workbook. Packed with activities, this workbook helps children engage with the story in a meaningful way. Download Your Free Workbook Here
https://karenbrough.com/register/

We'd Love Your Feedback!

Your thoughts and reviews help us reach more readers
and continue creating stories that touch hearts.
If you enjoyed our books, please take a moment
to leave a quick star review or comment.

Made in the USA
Las Vegas, NV
22 November 2024